Service
with a Smile

Published by Ron Kaufman Pte Ltd. - 10 9 8 7 6 5 4 3 2

Lift Me Up! - Service with a Smile
ISBN 981-05-2927-9 - 136 pages

1. Customer Service   2. Quotations
3. Self-Help   4. Ron Kaufman   5. Title

Cover and page layout by The Bonsey Design Partnership.
Cover illustrations by Ngu Hie Ling.
Set in Times and Arial fonts. Printed in Singapore.

Every effort has been made to credit the original author and make full acknowledgement of the source for each quotation in this text. However, if you know of any instance where the quotation or citation could be more accurate, please send a message to Ron@RonKaufman.com Any corrections will gladly be included in future editions. Thank you.

Below each attributed quotation are **quips, quotes and anecdotes in bold text**. These additional notes are by Ron Kaufman (1956 –), who should be cited as the author in all future works.

Ron Kaufman, Lift Me Up!, Pick Me Up!, UP Your Service!, and a balloon with the word 'UP' are registered trademarks of Ron Kaufman Pte Ltd.

Additional copies of this book are available at discount for promotional events, contests, awards and in-house training programs. For details and fast delivery, contact:

Ron Kaufman Pte Ltd   Tel: (+65) 6441-2760
50 Bayshore Park #31-01   Fax: (+65) 6444-8292
Aquamarine Tower   Ron@RonKaufman.com
Singapore 469977   www.RonKaufman.com

Contents

Service counts

In business today, service is not an issue: if you don't provide service, you're out of business.

John Bell

Customer experience is the next competitive battleground. It's where business is going to be won or lost.

Tom Knighton

Service is not optional, it's essential.

It's time to compete for your customers. Are you ready to win?

Be it furniture, clothes or health care, many industries today are marketing nothing more than commodities – no more, no less. What will make the difference in the long run is the care and feeding of customers.

Michael Mescon

You'll never have a product or price advantage again. They can be too easily duplicated. But a strong customer service culture can't be copied.

Jerry Fritz

Feed your customers well and they'll return for a second serving.

If they can't match you, they can't catch you.

It's delighted customers who carry the greatest clout for your promotion, your prosperity and your future.

Ron Kaufman

The principle was right there – you couldn't miss it. The more we did for our customers, the more they did for us.

Debbi Fields

Delighted customers are the only advertisement everyone believes.

Give as much as you can to your customers and they'll give much to you.

There are only two ways to get a new customer: 1. Solicit a new customer any way you can. 2. Take good care of your present customers so they don't become someone else's new customers.

Ed Zeitz

We shall serve for the joy of serving. Prosperity shall flow to us and through us in unending streams of plenty.

Charles Fillmore

The more you do #2, the less you'll need #1.

Serve because you want to. Succeed because you choose to.

It is well worth remembering that the customer is the most important factor in any business. If you don't think so, try getting along without him for a while.

Napoleon Hill

The customer is why you go to work. If they go away, you do, too.

David Haverford

What would a business be without customers?

A business existing for its own sake risks failing. A business existing for its customer's sake risks succeeding.

The purpose of a business is to create and keep customers.

Theodore Levitt

One hundred minus one can't be ninety-nine in the hotel business. It may be zero. If one employee out of hundreds gives a bad impression to a certain customer, it will be one hundred percent damage for our hotel image for that customer.

Ichiro Inumaru

A product is a starting point. A loyal customer is the goal.

One person can make all the difference – for better or for worse.

In the world of internet customer service, it's important to remember – your competitor is only one mouse click away.

Doug Warner

Revolve your world around the customer and more customers will revolve around you.

Heather Williams

The competition has never been closer.

What does your world revolve around?

Do *you* know what's best for customers? Or do you listen to what customers say they want? That could be the best thing for you.

Ron Kaufman

Merely satisfying your customers is no longer enough to ensure you receive their praise and future business.

Janelle Barlow

The business that listens is the business that learns.

Satisfaction is the least that is expected. Is that the least you can do?

More business is lost every year through neglect than through any other cause.

Jim Cathcart

I don't want to do business with those who don't make a profit, because they can't give the best service.

Richard Bach

If you neglect your customers, they will neglect you.

Service comes at a price. You need to pay the price to make a profit.

Men are rich only as
they give. He who
gives great service gets
great returns.

Elbert Hubbard

Quality is remembered
long after the price is
forgotten.

Gucci slogan

**An investment in great
service is the most sure
to pay you back.**

**Price is just a number.
It's the quality that
counts.**

The man who will use his skill and constructive imagination to see how much he can give for a dollar, instead of how little he can give for a dollar, is bound to succeed.

Henry Ford

The clear road to success: create more value for customers.

If you could change anything about the way you approach selling, the thing that would make the biggest difference is your attitude – your attitude toward your customers, your service, the benefits of your products, your employer and yourself.

Dan Burt

A change in attitude changes everything.

The fundamental aim is to make money by satisfying customers.

John Egan

If you're not serving the customer, you'd better be serving someone who is.

Karl Albrecht

Make money today and you will do well today. Make money pleasing customers today and you will also do well tomorrow.

Serve your colleagues well so that they can serve your customers.

If you don't care, your customer never will.

Marlene Blaszczyk

Worry about being better; bigger will take care of itself. Think one customer at a time. Take care of each one the best way you can.

Gary Comer

To create customers that care, provide good customer care.

Before you satisfy many, learn to delight each one.

Everything starts with the customer.

Lou Gerstner

Every company's greatest assets are its customers, because without customers there is no company.

Michael LeBoeuf

A business is supported on a solid foundation of customers.

Give your greatest assets the greatest importance.

The customer is the
final inspector.

Steve Jobs

The extra mile will have
no traffic jams.

Anonymous

**How will your customers
rate you?**

**When you do a little
more, you stand out a lot
more.**

Goodwill is the only asset competition cannot undersell or destroy.

Marshall Field

The asset that cannot be destroyed is worth more than all the others.

Show me a business not guided by the idea that 'he profits most who serves best' and I will show you an outfit that is dead or dying.

B.F. Harris

Service does not exist at the expense of your profits. Profit exists because you made the investment in service.

The consumer is not a moron. She is your wife.

David Ogilvy

Being on par in terms of price and quality only gets you into the game. Service wins the game.

Tony Alessandra

To gain the consumers' respect, treat them with respect.

If you're competing to win, you need service on your side.

There is only one boss: the customer. And he can fire everybody in the company from the chairman on down, simply by spending his money somewhere else.

Sam Walton

One customer, well-taken-care-of, could be more valuable than $10,000 worth of advertising.

Jim Rohn

Never underestimate the power of your customers.

Treat every customer like your greatest asset. He or she could be.

Treat each customer as if they sign your paycheck. They do.

John Tscholl

If we don't take care of our customers, someone else will.

Ed Mitchell

Money only flows from the wallets of customers who are willing.

To protect yourself from competition, keep your customers close.

When you serve the customer better, there's always a return on your investment.

Kara Parlin

After-sales service is more important than assistance before sales. It is through such service that one gets permanent customers.

Konosuke Matsushita

A failing business thinks it costs too much to provide superior service. A successful business knows it costs too much not to.

It's what you do 'after the deal' that brings you the next one.

No company has a permanent consumer franchise. No one has the only game in town. The never-ending cycle of destruction and change inherent in a capitalist economy always provides new opportunities for those with determination, goals and concentration.

Harvey Mackay

Customers' voices are more precious than management guide-books.

Munetsugu Ichiban-ya

Where some see change and instability, others see endless opportunity.

The words your customers speak are expert suggestions.

'Adding value' is a key to business success. But don't assume all customers value the same thing! Take the time to interview and ask. They'll be glad you did. So will you.

Ron Kaufman

Give the world the best you have and the best will come back to you.

Madeline Bridges

To add value, you must first know what's valuable.

If you want to be the best, give the best.

Rule #1: The customer is always right.
Rule #2: If the customer is wrong, see Rule #1.

Stew Leonard

I consider each customer as a family member who deserves nothing but the best service.

Tammy Toh

Rule #3: If you can't remember the rules, ask your customers. They'll remind you.

When you serve another person, you share a moment in life. Honor it.

People don't buy because they understand. They buy because they feel understood.

Tan Suee Chieh

This principle applies in business and in life: When you give enough, then you will receive.

Ron Kaufman

First step: understand your customers. Second step: make sure they feel it.

It's easy to test this principle. Start giving, and keep on giving.

Make a customer,
not a sale.

Katherine Barchetti

Service is the rent we
pay for the privilege of
living on this earth.

Shirley Chisholm

**Each sale happens once.
Each customer can last
a lifetime.**

**Pay in advance – and
pay in full.**

It is one of the most beautiful compensations in life, that no man can sincerely try to help another without helping himself.

Ralph Waldo Emerson

Taking care of others is a good way to take care of yourself.

We don't want to push our ideas onto customers, we simply want to make what they want.

Laura Ashley

Choose your challenge: Spend time finding out what they want or spend *more* time trying to sell them what you've got.

Service is the currency that keeps our economy moving. I serve you in one business, you serve me in another. When either of us improves, the economy gets a little better. When both of us improve, people are sure to take notice. When everyone improves, the whole world grows stronger and closer together.

Ron Kaufman

Serving is an action that starts a chain reaction.

A customer you keep is one customer you don't have to find.

Shelley Wake

A customer not served is a customer not deserved.

The customer is why we are here. If we take good care of them, they'll give us good reason to come back.

Jenny McKenzie

Giving service is a form of self-interest for the person who does the serving.

Elbert Hubbard

Each customer you serve will bring more customers to you, or block customers from you. The choice is yours.

You do more for yourself when you forget yourself.

Once you shape a company to service the marketplace and your services are necessary, the company develops a compulsion of its own to grow.

Liz Claiborne

You always have to give 100 percent, because if you don't, someone, someplace, *will* give 100 percent and they will beat you when you meet.

Ed Macauley

The company that services someone's need, need not worry about serving its own.

Is 100 percent sufficient? Who will give more?

To give real service you must add something which cannot be bought or measured with money, and that is sincerity and integrity.

Douglas Adams

People forget how fast you did a job, but they remember how well you did it.

Howard Newton

The things you give that can't be measured are things that matter most.

Doing a fast job can impress for a short time. Doing a great job can impress for a lifetime.

Not too long ago, if you did things 75 percent right, it was okay. Now, if you don't do things 99 percent right, some competitor will eat you for lunch.

John Spoelhof

The bitterness of poor quality remains long after low pricing is forgotten.

Leon Cautillo

Do things 100 percent right and people will take you to lunch, not make you the lunch!

A low price is no excuse for low quality.

I'm not a driven businessman, but a driven artist. I never think about money. Beautiful things make money.

Geoffrey Beene

The question is, then, do we try to make things easy on ourselves or do we try to make things easy on our customers, whoever they may be?

Erwin Frand

Do what you're driven to do. The results will drive themselves.

How hard will you work to make it easy for your customers?

We make a living from what we get. We make a life from what we give.

Winston Churchill

If you don't genuinely like your customers, chances are they won't buy.

Tom Watson

We need a living and a life. But a good living is taken care of when you make a good life.

When you really care about your customers, you don't have to think about being 'caring'.

Consumers are statistics. Customers are people.

Stanley Marcus

Always think of your customers as suppliers first. Work closely with them, so they can supply *you* with the information you need to supply *them* with the right products and services.

Susan Marthaller

If you reduce your customers to numbers, your statistics will go in the same direction.

Knowledge is power. Treat your customers as the ultimate power source.

I don't know what your destiny will be, but one thing I do know: The only ones among you who will be really happy are those who have sought and found a way to serve.

Albert Schweitzer

Service is what life is all about.

Marian Edelman

The truly happy don't ask for help, they ask how they can help.

Serve well, do well.

If you do not look after today's business then you might as well forget about tomorrow.

Isaac Mophatlane

What goes around, comes around. What you send out *does* come back. Service is a two-way street. Life is, too.

Ron Kaufman

Plan for the future, but act in the present.

When you increase your output, the input will take care of itself.

Service improvement

I use nothing but the best ingredients. My cookies are always baked fresh. I price cookies so that you cannot make them at home for any less. And I still give cookies away.

Debbi Fields

Be outrageous!
It's the only place that isn't crowded.

Ron Kaufman

Be irresistible!
Be the best you can be in every possible way.

Outrageous actions can lead to outrageous results.

In case of rain, protect your customers with your umbrella and walk them to their cars.

Toyota sales manual

If one of our customers comes into the store without a smile, I'll give them one of mine.

Sam Walton

When an opportunity arises to show your customers you care, take it!

If customers leave without a purchase, you have not failed. But if customers leave without a smile, you have.

A smile is the light in your window that tells others that there is a caring, sharing person inside.

Denis Waitley

Reaching out takes nothing more than a smile.

Double-check your voice mail message. Listen to your on-hold words and music. Write welcoming scripts for your telephone team. Pay attention to the music in your office and lobby areas. Make sure what your customers hear *sounds* good.

Ron Kaufman

How does your customer hear you?

Unless you have 100 percent customer satisfaction... you must improve.

Horst Schulz

Quality isn't something that can be promised into an article. It must be put there. If it isn't put there, the finest sales talk in the world won't act as a substitute.

C.G. Campbell

Always aim for 100 percent and you'll always know where to improve.

Quality is more than a promise, it's genuine performance.

Customer complaints
are the schoolbooks
from which we learn.

Lou Gerstner

Customers don't expect
you to be perfect. They
do expect you to fix
things when they go
wrong.

Donald Porter

**How can you learn
more? By admiring what
you've done right? Or by
studying what you've
done wrong?**

**Making an honest
mistake is acceptable.
Failing to fix it is not.**

Without great employees you can never have great customer service. •

Richard Gerson

Motivate them, train them, care about them and make winners out of them. We know if we treat our employees right, they'll treat the customers right. And if customers are treated right, they'll come back.

J.W. Marriot, Jr.

Developing great employees attracts great customers.

Employees are the key to your success with customers. Treat them well!

When the alarm bell rings, you'd better wake up and realize that the customer expects more from you today than he did the day before. You'd better find ways to be better.

Gary Tooker

Don't wait for the alarm bell to ring.

The *best* customer is the one that complains. Nice customers just go away without telling you. Ninety-six percent of unhappy customers are silent. But they cost you millions.

Chang Yu Sang

Silent customers can be deadly. *Encourage* them to complain.

Sell practical, tested merchandise at a reasonable profit, treat your customers like human beings and they will always come back.

L.L. Bean

Ask your loyal customers for positive comments about your products and your service. Then post these testimonials where other customers and prospects can enjoy them.

Ron Kaufman

If you were a customer, would you come back to buy *your* products or services?

Testimonials describe what has been, and are a promise of what is to come.

We consistently seek out very demanding customers, which challenges us to perform even better.

Suresh Sundram

Here is a simple but powerful rule: Always give people more than they expect to get.

Nelson Boswell

If your customers are demanding, be thankful.

If customers say you're just 'all right', you've not done enough, you've failed to delight.

Being sincere and honest, my father treats his customers like friends. He tells his customers frankly what is the right choice for them rather than trying to make the most profit out of them.

Supon Pornnirunlit

Nothing is more harmful to the service, than the neglect of discipline; for that discipline, more than numbers, gives one army superiority over another.

George Washington

Think of what is best for them, not what is best for you.

You can't control how everyone will feel. But discipline controls what everyone will do.

Quality is everyone's responsibility.

W. Edwards Deming

The most effective way to achieve right relations with any living thing is to look for the best in it, and then help that best into the fullest expression.

Allen Boone

Is *everyone* playing their part?

If you want to be the best, find the best in others.

Thou ought to be nice, even to superstition, in keeping thy promises, and therefore equally cautious in making them.

Thomas Fuller

The man who promises everything is sure to fulfill nothing, and everyone who promises too much is in danger of using evil means to carry out his promises, and is already on the road to perdition.

Carl Jung

Words not kept break more than a promise.

Promise too much and you'll have plenty of room to fail. Promise little and you'll have plenty of room to excel.

53

Never say no when a client asks for something, even if it is the moon. You can always try, and anyhow there is plenty of time afterwards to explain that it was not possible.

Cesar Ritz

Good business leaders create a vision, articulate the vision, passionately own the vision and relentlessly drive it to completion.

John Welch

If it's not impossible, you may as well try. If it *is* impossible, at least you'll find out why.

A great leader makes what is visible in their mind, visible to all.

When the customer makes contact, he does not want a quote. He wants a commitment.

Ron Kaufman

You can start right where you stand and apply the habit of going the extra mile by rendering more service and better service than you are being paid for.

Napoleon Hill

Without commitment, no price will be low enough. With commitment, no price will be too high.

The starting point is always now. The end is up to you.

It's not what you do once in a while, it's what you do day in and day out that makes the difference.

Jenny Craig

You can't promise your customers sunny weather, but you can promise to hold an umbrella over them when it rains.

Ron Zemke

Constant acts of goodness are worth far more than rare acts of greatness.

Always do what you can do instead of worrying about what you can't.

It's not about scale, it's about the depth of the relationship. It's not so much the share-of-market that's important, but the share-of-customer.

Ian Kennedy

All people smile in the same language.

Anne Frank

The right measure is not how many customers you've got, but how closely you hold them.

Crossing barriers can be as simple as a smile.

No one needs a smile as much as a person who fails to give one.

Rebecca Kaufman

To be prepared is half the victory.

Miguel de Cervantes

If you only give back what you get from other people, you're not giving as much as you can.

Are you prepared to win?

Spectacular achievement
is always preceded by
spectacular preparation.

Robert Schuller

In our factory, we make
lipstick. In our
advertising, we sell
hope.

Charles Revlon

**Preparation clears a
pathway for success.**

**What does your product
really mean to the
people who buy it?**

Quality in a service or product is not what you put into it. It's what the client or customer gets out of it.

Peter Drucker

When things go wrong, your best *recovery effort* is required. But don't just provide the missing piece (that's the *recovery*), also provide uniquely personal assistance (that's the memorable *effort*).

Ron Kaufman

The true measure of what you put in, is what's received on the other end.

Every service problem is as an opportunity to show you care.

Occasionally problems will occur. When it happens to your customers, fix the problem *fast*. Make it your speed and generosity that gets remembered, not the problem.

Ron Kaufman

Hire people who are better than you are, then leave them to get on with it. Look for people who will aim for the remarkable, who will not settle for the routine.

David Ogilvy

If they're going to remember the problem, make sure they remember it fondly.

If you want to be the best, find the best, hire the best – and let them do their best.

The best morale exists when you never hear the word mentioned. When you hear a lot of talk about it, it's usually lousy.

Dwight D. Eisenhower

A well-informed employee is the best salesperson a company can have.

Edwin Thomas

Things that are obvious don't need to be talked about. Things that are missing, do.

When your staff are 'information-rich', their information can make *you* rich!

Outstanding leaders go out of their way to boost the self-esteem of their personnel. When people believe in themselves, it's amazing what they can accomplish.

Sam Walton

An acre of performance is worth a whole world of promise.

William Howells

Be the mirror in which people admire their true potential.

Say it with words. Show it with action.

Wise are those who learn that the bottom line doesn't always have to be their top priority.

William Ward

Do not confuse motion and progress. A rocking horse keeps moving but does not make any progress.

Alfred Montapert

The bottom line is a by-product of taking care of your main product – your customers.

Are you moving forward, or just moving?

Unless commitment is made, there are only promises and hopes, but no plans.

Peter Drucker

Eighty percent of success is showing up.

Woody Allen

Plans turn promises into results and dreams into realities.

The first step to delighting your customers is being there when they need you.

Behave toward everyone as if you are receiving a great guest.

Confucius

Delay is the deadliest form of denial.

Northcote Parkinson

Because you are!

Procrastination is the beginning of poor performance.

Indecision and delay
are the parents of
failure.

George Canning

Efficiency is doing
things right;
effectiveness is doing
the right things.

Peter Drucker

**It's fine to wait for an
appropriate time, but it's
inappropriate to wait
forever.**

**First be effective and
then be efficient.**

To aim is not enough,
you must make contact.

German proverb

Our goal is perfection.
Excellence will be
tolerated.

Sim Kay Wee

**Preparation is good, but
customers need results.**

**Make your upper limit,
no limit.**

If you don't focus,
you'll spray.

Ron Kaufman

Confidence is
contagious – so is
lack of confidence.

Michael O'Brien

A scattered effort is a poor effort.

Be confident enough to encourage confidence in others.

Use your good judgment in all situations. There will be no additional rules.

Nordstrom's employee manual

Reason alone is insufficient to make us enthusiastic in any matter.

François de La Rochefoucauld

Are people being the least you expect of them, or the best they expect themselves to be?

Convince people and you win their minds. Inspire people and you win their hearts.

You can work with people more successfully by engaging their feelings than by convincing their reason.

Paul Parker

Shall we make a new rule of life from tonight: always to try to be a little kinder than is necessary?

J.M. Barrie

If you want to interest people, make them think. If you want to inspire people, make them feel.

Are you doing only what you must or doing all you can?

A person who trusts other people will make fewer mistakes than the person who distrusts them.

Camillo di Cavour

Set your expectations high; find men and women whose integrity and values you respect; get their agreement on a course of action; and give them your ultimate trust.

John Akers

Always trust people and they may let you down. Always distrust people and you have let them down.

If you haven't given them your trust, you haven't given them enough.

Trust is the lubrication that makes it possible for organizations to work.

Warren Bennis

Competition is like cod liver oil. First it makes you sick, then it makes you better.

Samuel Kaufman

Only a well-oiled machine runs smoothly.

When something needs to be improved, take your medicine – fix it.

We must expect to fail. But fail in a learning posture, determined not to repeat the mistakes. Then maximize benefits from what you can learn in the process.

Ted Engstrom

There are two ways to improve your service, and yourself: maximize your strengths and minimize your weaknesses.

Ron Kaufman

Every failure counts.

Tend your own garden: savor the blossoms, trim the weeds.

Everyone needs to be valued. Everyone has the potential to give something back.

Ron Kaufman

Pleasure in the job puts perfection in the work.

Aristotle

The most valuable person is the one who cherishes the value in others.

Enjoy your work so that others may enjoy the results.

A good plan, vigorously executed now, is better than a perfect plan next week.

George Patton

I have yet to find the person who did not do better work and put forth greater effort under a spirit of approval than under a spirit of criticism.

Charles Schwab

In a service situation, each delay can mean many unsatisfied customers, each one telling many more.

Your approval gives others the confidence to serve, to learn, to try.

I consider my ability to arouse enthusiasm among people the greatest asset I possess.

Charles Schwab

One machine can do the work of 50 ordinary people. No machine can do the work of one extraordinary person.

Elbert Hubbard

Enthusiastic service providers create enthusiastic customers.

Be extraordinary!

I would rather be surrounded by smart people than have a huge budget. Smart people will get you there faster.

Ethan Rasiel

When you train people properly, they won't be able to tell the difference between role-play and the real thing. If anything, the real thing will be easier.

Richard Marcinko

Money has a fixed value. People can have unlimited value.

You can't always hire great service providers, but you can create them.

It is surprising what people can do when they have to, and how little most will do when they don't have to.

Walter Linn

In hiring people, look for three qualities: integrity, intelligence and energy. But if they don't have the first, the other two will kill you.

Warren Buffett

Create a compelling service vision. When people want to, they will.

Intelligence is useful. Energy is valuable. Integrity is essential.

A thousand words will not leave so deep an impression as one deed.

Henrik Ibsen

Don't just talk about it, do it.

Do the right thing. It will gratify some people and astonish the rest.

Mark Twain

Do what's right and you'll never go wrong.

Have a bias toward action – let's see something happen now. Break that big plan into small steps and take the first step right away.

Richard Thalheimer

Stop looking for the 'X' factor. Build it!

Ron Kaufman

Even a tiny step is one step closer to where you're going.

You can't find what doesn't exist, but you can create it.

Price is what you pay.
Value is what you get.

Warren Buffett

Quality is never an accident; it is always the result of high intention, sincere effort, intelligent direction and skillful execution; it represents the wise choice of many alternatives.

William Foster

Customers pay a price, but they remember the value.

Quality is a choice. Choose to make it better.

The only way to know how customers see your business is to look at it through their eyes.

Daniel Scroggin

People expect a certain response from a business. When you pleasantly exceed those expectations you've passed an important psychological threshold.

Richard Thalheimer

To see like a customer, be like a customer.

Exceeding expectations is where satisfaction ends and loyalty begins.

Excellence is doing
ordinary things
extraordinarily well.

John Gardner

Much good work is lost
for the lack of a little
more commitment.

Edward Harriman

**Everything ordinary has
the potential to be
extraordinary.**

**Many good customers
are lost that way, too.**

Anybody who accepts mediocrity – in school, on the job, in life – is one who compromises. When a leader compromises, the whole organization compromises.

Charles Knight

Excellence is the result of always striving to do better.

Pat Riley

Compromise in your arguments, not in your expectations.

Let today's strong performance be your starting point for tomorrow.

People are more important than tools. If you don't believe so, put a good tool into the hands of a poor worker.

John Bernet

Vision without action is a daydream. Action without vision is a nightmare.

Japanese proverb

Giving great service requires the right people *and* the right service tools.

Vision *with* action makes a powerful reality.

There are three levels of vision:
1. What's do-able
2. What's conceivable
3. What was previously unthinkable.

Anthony Yeo

What's possible today isn't bound by what was possible yesterday, and is never a measure of what's possible tomorrow.

A promise is most given when least is said.

George Chapman

Your promise means more than the words you use to give it.

Your customers get
better when you do.

Bill Gates

The single most
important thing to
remember about any
enterprise is that there
are no results inside its
walls. The result of a
successful business is a
satisfied customer.

Peter Drucker

**The better you perform,
the better off they'll be.**

**Your profits reflect the
success of your
customers.**

When you start viewing your customers as interruptions, you're going to have problems.

Kate Zabriskie

Don't just learn the tricks of the trade. Learn the trade.

James Bennis

If you turn your back on a customer, you turn your back on success.

Service skills are the foundation for your success.

No institution can survive if it needs geniuses to manage it. It must be organized to be able to get along under a leadership composed of average human beings.

Peter Drucker

A good business knows what the customer wants. A great business shows the customer what they didn't yet know they wanted.

Shelley Wake

Make your service systems so strong that everyone looks like a genius.

Give your customers what they want today, and help them see tomorrow.

Strong cash flow hides many sins.

Wyn Dunford

Sometimes we become so expert in our own domain, we forget that customers may be less familiar.

Ron Kaufman

Service sins don't stay hidden and eventually weaken the cash flow.

'Industry jargon' may not be a language your customer understands.

Service attitude

A customer who complains is my best friend.

Stew Leonard

Who sets your standards – your industry, your ego or your customers?

Harry Beckwith

Hearing what you've done right is valuable. Hearing what you've done wrong can be priceless.

Which standards do you use for your business?

The person who sees a need and wants to be asked to help is as unkind as the person who refused to give it.

Dante Alighieri

He gives twice who gives promptly.

Publilius Syrus

Acting after being asked is compliance. Acting without being asked is kindness.

When you see the need, take the action.

I expect to pass through life but once. If there be any kindness I can show, or any good thing I can do for any fellow being, let me do it now, as I shall not pass this way again.

William Penn

Everyone has an invisible sign hanging from their neck saying, 'Please make me feel important.' Remember this message when working with people.

Mary Kay Ash

Don't wait. Tomorrow may be too late to do the things you can today.

You are as important as you make others feel.

Beginning today, treat everyone you meet as if they were going to be dead by midnight. Extend to them all the care, kindness and understanding you can muster, and do it with no thought of any reward. Your life will never be the same again.

Og Mandino

Performance is your reality. Forget everything else.

Harold Geneen

How much good can you do today? How much love can you give? How much care and kind attention?

What matters more? What you said you'd do, what you hoped to do, or what you did?

There are two types of people – those who come into a room and say, 'Well, here I am!' and those who come in and say, 'Ah, there you are.'

Frederick Collins

Whatever happens, take responsibility.

Anthony Robbins

Let your *customers* say, 'Well, here I am,' while *you* say, 'There you are!'

You cannot change what has already happened. You can always change the way you respond.

Nothing strengthens the judgment and quickens the conscience like individual responsibility.

Elizabeth Stanton

A professional is someone who can do his best work when he doesn't feel like it.

Alistair Cooke

You are the person who determines what you do. That's a big responsibility. Make the most of it.

Passion isn't always available. The committed get things done even without it.

Well done is better than well said.

Benjamin Franklin

We cannot live for ourselves alone. Our lives are connected by a thousand invisible threads. Along these sympathetic fibers, our actions run as causes and return to us as results.

Herman Melville

Your value is not determined by your words, but by how well you live up to them.

For every life, there is a flow. The more you ask, the more you'll know. The more you give, the more you'll grow.

Kindness in words
creates confidence.
Kindness in thinking
creates profundity.
Kindness in giving
creates love.

Lao Tzu

Everybody can be great
because anybody can
serve. You don't have
to have a college
degree to serve. You
don't have to make
your subject and verb
agree to serve. You
only need a heart full of
grace. A soul generated
by love.

Martin Luther King, Jr.

**Always be kind in your
heart, spirit and mind.**

**The measure of
greatness is not how
much you have got, but
how much you are willing
to give.**

It is easier to do a job right than to explain why you didn't.

Martin Van Buren

Avoid the hassle – get it right the first time.

Be unselfish. That is the first and final commandment for those who would be useful, and happy in their usefulness.

Charles Eliot

Life is not a solitary activity. Live well by living for others.

Do right. Do your best.
Treat others as you
want to be treated.

Lou Holtz

The measure of a man
is not the number of his
servants, but the number
of people whom he
serves.

Paul Moody

**What is the most you
would do for yourself?
Offer the same to
others.**

**If you want to live more,
give more.**

Always do more than is
required of you.

George Patton

In the time we have, it
is surely our duty to do
all the good we can to
all the people we can in
all the ways we can.

William Barclay

**Meeting expectations is
good. Exceeding
expectations is better.**

**Every day is an
opportunity to make a
difference. What will you
do today?**

Joy can be real only if people look on their life as a service, and have a definite object in life outside themselves and their personal happiness.

Leo Tolstoy

It is when we forget ourselves that we do things which will be remembered.

Rebecca Kaufman

Joy is not a goal, it's the outcome of reaching for worthy service goals.

Focus not on who you are, but on what you can do for others.

And ofttimes excusing
of a fault doth make
the fault the worse by
the excuse.

William Shakespeare

Bad excuses are worse
than none.

Thomas Fuller

**When things go wrong,
make improvements, not
excuses.**

**Tell the truth. If there is
no good reason, don't
make one up.**

Do your work; not just your work and no more, but a little more for the lavishing's sake – that little more which is worth all the rest.

Dean Briggs

I am seeking, I am striving, I am in it with all my heart.

Vincent van Gogh

Don't let doing enough be good enough.

You can only achieve the most you are striving for.

We distinguish the excellent man from the common man by saying that the former is the one who makes great demands on himself, and the latter who makes no demands on himself.

José Ortega y Gasset

In all human affairs there are efforts and there are results, and the strength of the effort is the measure of the result.

James Allen

Ask more from yourself and you will get more. Demand more from yourself and you will achieve more.

Unlimited efforts can produce unlimited results.

Enthusiasm is like
having two right hands.

Elbert Hubbard

The principle is
competing with your-
self. It's all about self
improvement, about
being better than you
were the day before.

Steve Young

**Unless you are left-
handed, in which case...**

**Don't aim for yesterday's
standards. Aim for the
standards of tomorrow.**

If you take responsibility for yourself you will develop a hunger to accomplish your dreams.

Les Brown

Action springs not from thought, but from a readiness for responsibility.

Dietrich Bonhoeffer

Dreams come true when we accept that they are ours to create.

Are you ready to act? Are you ready to succeed?

Nobody made a greater
mistake than he who
did nothing because he
could do only a little.

Edmund Burke

No one ever listened
themselves out of a job.

Calvin Coolidge

**When only a little can be
done, doing it becomes
the greatest you can do.**

**You've got one mouth
and two ears. There's a
reason.**

The greatest gift you can give another is the purity of your attention.

Richard Moss

A powerful man makes every other man feel small. But a great man makes every other man feel great.

Gilbert Chesterton

Attention is measured in quality not quantity.

Greatness is not how you feel, it's how you make others feel.

May I never get too busy in my own affairs that I fail to respond to the needs of others with kindness and compassion.

Thomas Jefferson

A successful person is one who can lay a firm foundation with the bricks that other people throw at him or her.

David Brinkley

How long does it take to be kind?

You can get hurt, get hidden or get stronger. You choose!

Sales are contingent upon the attitude of the salesman, not the attitude of the prospect.

W. Clement Stone

Look in the face of the person to whom you are speaking if you wish to know his real sentiments, for he can command his words more easily than his countenance.

Lord Chesterfield

Good attitudes are contagious. Make yours worth catching!

Listen to customers and you will hear them. Look carefully at customers and you will see them. Do both and you will understand them.

Strive not to be a success, but rather to be of value.

Albert Einstein

I do not think there is any other quality so essential to success as perseverance. It overcomes almost everything, even nature.

John D. Rockefeller

What you want to be defines what you become.

Could you achieve the possible without trying? Could you achieve the impossible if you refuse to stop trying?

One of the rarest things a man ever does is to do the best he can.

Josh Billings

Keep doing good deeds long enough, and you'll probably turn out a good man in spite of yourself.

Louis Auchincloss

Be the exception to the rule. It's the surest way to become exceptional.

To be good, do good.

You cannot hope to build a better world without improving the individuals. To that end, each of us must work for our own improvement and, at the same time, share a general responsibility for all humanity, our particular duty being to aid those to whom we think we can be most useful.

Marie Curie

The true meaning of life is to plant trees under whose shade you do not expect to sit.

Nelson Henderson

What is an organization? What is a family? What is our world? We are a collection of individuals, all sharing life together.

Selfless acts are a source of profound meaning for your self and your life.

He who excuses himself, accuses himself.

Gabriel Meurier

Resolve to make each day the very best and don't let anyone get in your way. If they do, step past them.

Ivan Benson

The shelter of excuses has a leaky roof.

Make each day another step in the right direction.

4

Service innovation

Service is the ultimate
edge. Keep it sharp.

Ron Kaufman

Business has only two
functions – marketing
and innovation.

Peter Drucker

**The cutting edge of
service is always being
honed and polished.**

**Create new ways to
serve your customers
(innovation), and better
ways to tell them about it
(marketing).**

The most damaging sentence in any language is: 'It's always been done that way.'

Grace Hopper

When was the last time you did something for the first time?

Thomas Edison

If you're always doing what you've always done, you'll never see (or become) what you could be!

Never rest on past success. Create something better.

You can't just ask customers what they want and then try to give that to them. By the time you get it built, they'll want something new.

Steve Jobs

In business, the competition will bite you if you keep running. If you stand still, they will swallow you.

William Knudsen

If your customers have to ask you for it, you haven't been thinking far enough ahead.

Run fast, run far, keep running!

We bring together the best ideas – turning the meetings of our top managers into intellectual orgies.

Jack Welch

If you want to be creative in your company, your career, your life, all it takes is one step: the extra one.

Dale Dauten

One idea creates an innovation. Many ideas create a transformation.

The only way to go further than you've been is to take an extra step.

Progress is a tide. If we stand still we will surely be drowned. To stay on the crest, we have to keep moving.

Harold Mayfield

Q: When you are already in the lead, how do you to stay ahead?

A: Set the pace and rule the race. Seek new ways to differentiate, new ways to surprise and delight your customers.

Ron Kaufman

Stay in one place too long and the tide can overwhelm you. Ride the tide, surf the waves, stay on top of the changes.

No matter how far you get ahead, someone's always chasing your customers. Someone's always chasing you!

If the rate of change on the outside exceeds the rate of change on the inside, the end is near.

Jack Welch

Test fast, fail fast, adjust fast.

Tom Peters

When customers' expectations change faster than your willingness or ability to serve them, you can be sure they'll be someone else's customers soon.

When was the last time you tried something different to please a customer? What's *your* speed of change?

Once a new technology rolls over you, if you're not part of the steamroller, you're part of the road.

Stewart Brand

Everything can be improved.

C. W. Barron

Flatten or be flattened. Use new technology to serve your customers better.

And your customers expect it!

When you're out of quality, you're out of business.

Philip Cosby

Good enough never is.

Debbi Fields

Good customers want good quality service. Great customers want it even more.

No one ever delighted a customer by being 'good enough'.

I do not believe you can do today's job with yesterday's methods and be in business tomorrow.

Nelson Jackson

If e-mail had been around before the telephone was invented, people would have said, 'Hey, forget e-mail! With this new telephone invention I can actually talk to people!'

Thomas Friedman

What you did in the past is how you got to today. What you do today is how you will get to the future.

Don't let high-speed completely replace high-touch. Your customers may appreciate both.

Create the 'possible' service; don't just create what the market needs or wants. Create what it would love.

Harry Beckwith

If people did not sometimes do silly things, nothing intelligent would ever get done.

Ludwig Wittgenstein

If you want to stay in business, satisfy customers. If you want to excel in business, delight customers.

Who could imagine *delivering* a pizza? Melted cheese on a motorcycle? The first person must have been crazy...and a genius.

There is a quality of mind which leads in making discoveries. It is the power of never letting exceptions go unnoticed.

Francis Darwin

You have to create a track record of breaking your own mold, or at least other people's idea of that mold.

William Hurt

When a customer asks what no one else has ever asked, pay close attention.

Are current expectations a standard or a challenge?

If you do things well, do them better. Be daring, be first, be different.

Anita Roddick

Change before you have to.

Jack Welch

There's no such thing as the very best. If you're doing your best, it's only because you haven't yet found a way to do better.

If you wait until you have to change, you may have waited too long.

Instead of seeing the rug being pulled from under you, learn to dance on a moving carpet.

Thomas Crum

The easier it is to do something, the harder it is to change the way you do it.

Steve Wozniak

You can't stop change. Don't let it it stop you.

Challenge your own status quo – before someone else does.

The only limits are, as always, those of vision.

James Broughton

The only sustainable competitive advantage comes from out-innovating the competition.

James Morse

Let your imagination soar. What you can do for customers is more than you see today.

If you want to outdo the competition, start by out-serving them.

There ain't no rules around here. We're trying to accomplish something.

Thomas Edison

We must not, in trying to think about how we can make a big difference, ignore the small daily differences we can make which, over time, add up to big differences that we often cannot foresee.

Marian Edelman

Rules impose limits. Do you want to limit your service achievements?

Big service achievements do not replace small service gestures.

The path of least resistance and least trouble is a mental rut already made. It requires troublesome work to undertake the alteration of old beliefs.

John Dewey

Questions focus our thinking. Ask yourself: What's good about this? What's not perfect about it yet? What can I do differently or better the next time?

Charles Connolly

Be willing to challenge your current beliefs. Even the best ideas fade with age.

You'll never find the answers if you never ask the questions.

If you think of standardization as the best you know today, but which will be improved tomorrow, you can get somewhere.

Henry Ford

We need to set our course by the stars, not by the lights of every passing ship.

Omar Bradley

Make 'continuous improvement' your standardization.

Success is constantly moving toward the steady goal of loyal and delighted customers.

Thank you for choosing this book! Among the 512 positive quotes, quips and action tips, this one is my favorite:

> I expect to pass through life but once. If there be any kindness I can show, or any good thing I can do for any fellow being, let me do it now, as I shall not pass this way again.
> – William Penn

Which quote do you enjoy the most? Who can you share it with in kindness today?

Wishing you a service with a smile!

To order more copies of the **Lift Me Up!**® books, visit your local bookstore or www.LiftMeUpBooks.com